TRACK PRINTS

A Photographic History of British Tanks of the Great War 1914-18

By
Richard Pullen

First Edition Published in 2009 by TUCANNbooks

ISBN 978-1-873257-99-9

Text and Pictures © Richard Pullen 2009.
Design © TUCANNbooks 2009

Produced by: TUCANNdesign&print, 19 High Street, Heighington, Lincoln LN4 1RG
Tel & Fax: 01522 790009
Website. www.tucann.co.uk

ABOUT THE AUTHOR

Richard Pullen has been a field archaeologist for almost fifteen years and although his particular interest is industrial archaeology, during his archaeological career he has directed sites of all periods throughout the British Isles. He gained a Masters Degree in Archaeology and Museum Management in late 2004 and he was one of the founder members of Friends of the Lincoln Tank.

Richard started writing in 2001 as a hobby, but has now been writing professionally for over five years. He has had four books and numerous articles published in this time.

Also by the same author

The Landships of Lincoln-Second Edition
The story of Lincolns part in the invention of the first Tanks 1915-1918

Beyond the Green Fields
*The final memories of some of the first men of the Tank Corps
as told in their own words*

Tanks of the Great War Colouring Book
An introduction into the world of Great War tanks for the younger enthusiast

Thanks, as always, must go to David Fletcher and Janice Tait from the Tank Museum, Bovington, for their help and endlessly cheerful assistance.

Several of the photographs used in this book came from the archive of the world renowned industrial historian, Ray Hooley and from the splendid collection of the late and much missed Bill Baker. Thank you Bill.

I must also thank Joanne, Grace, Hannah, William and Avro for being there when I needed them.

This book is dedicated to the 'Lost Generation'.

To the men of all countries who went to war in the first tanks, not to take life, but in an attempt to end the stalemate, break the trenches and cut short a war.

LEST WE FORGET.

INTRODUCTION

In 1914 war broke out and for the first time in history, war was being fought between major world superpowers. Up until now, large countries with modern mechanized armies preferred to fight small wars against indigenous people who were armed with little more than spears and clubs. This new 'World War' meant that neither side had a material or military advantage over the enemy.

The huge professional German army of 1914 were geared up for all out war and soon had the relatively tiny British Expeditionary Force on the back-foot. In order to save the majority of the BEF the unfortunate, but sensible decision was taken to begin the retreat to Mons. Unfortunately, this lead to another inevitable, but even more regrettable decision and the BEF started to 'dig in'. Soon, the Allies had the better position and were relatively well protected in their foxholes. The training and discipline of the British rifleman would now pay dividends and they began to mow the oncoming Germans down with such ferocity that the previously undisturbed wheat fields were soon *'grey with piles of hundreds German dead'*. Before long, the German army were forced to follow suit by also digging in and soon the shallow fox holes of 1914 had become a huge network of trenches which snaked across France and Belgium from the Channel Ports to the Alps. The Western Front had become a filthy, corpse ridden morass of mud and barbed wire. Every day, more and more trench mortars, machine-guns and Howitzers arrived in Flanders and before long the Great War had become deadlocked. Neither army could cross no-man's land and if they tried, the machine guns would cut them to pieces with terrifying efficiency. By 1916 things had gone about as far as they could go and an answer to the endless *'Riddle of the Trenches'* needed to be found as soon as possible if the war was not to continue on into the 1920s.

The invention that eventually changed all of this was the Tank and on 15th September 1916 it made its debut on the sodden battlefield of the Somme. Unfortunately, the original Mark I Tank was not an instant hit and its initial debut at Flers on the Somme was hardly a terrific success. The new weapon was used in small numbers and on unsuitable ground; these were lessons which were sorely learnt by those who sent the tanks into battle. The awful ground conditions and mechanical teething problems meant that the Mk I did not perform as well as had been hoped. Over the next two years, the tank would evolve and the first Mk I would develop into the excellent and incredibly useful Mk V**. It was probably as the Mk IV at The Battle of Cambrai that the Great War tank had its finest hour. On 20th November 1917 the newly formed Tank Corps took their Mk IV machines into battle at Cambrai in large numbers and on good ground. At that famous battle the tanks and their supporting infantry secured an initial advance of over six miles. Unfortunately, the tanks gains were not properly exploited and the battle ended as a virtual draw. Despite this disappointing end to a promising advance, Church bells were rung in England to celebrate the terrific success of the tanks.

The creation of a viable tank in 1916 was a culmination of ideas and inventions going back over 3000 years. Several people had tried to create an armoured vehicle that could go over rough ground and was impervious to enemy fire, but it was not until William Foster and Co Ltd of Lincoln England got involved in 1915 that the 3000 year old idea of the tank finally became a reality.

In 1915, Fosters of Lincoln were building the Foster Daimler 105hp Tractor for the Admiralty. After several different prototypes, this excellent machine would eventually become the basis of their next invention, known at the time as a Landship. The Landship project was a great success and Fosters work on it lead directly to the arrival of the tank on the battlefield. The work undertaken at the factory by William Tritton, Walter Wilson, William Rigby and the rest of the design team and workforce cannot be underestimated. They were asked to produce a tracked armoured fighting vehicle from a half thought out idea at a time when the relevant technology to do so hardly existed.

The Tank was unlike anything anyone had ever seen before. It seemed to have no driver, there were no wheels, no horses and it made a terrible, unearthly clatter as it trundled along in a cloud of smoke at its maximum speed of around 4mph. This ghostly apparition obviously captured the undivided attention of anyone who came across it. The Allies saw the new machine as the mythical war winning weapon they had been waiting for and the Germans saw it, at first anyway, as nothing short of the Devil himself. Soon the Germans horror turned to fascination as they explored the tanks true strengths and weaknesses. The Germans went to great lengths to catalogue and photograph any and all damaged, ditched or knocked out machines they found on the battlefield.

The tank would also capture the imagination of the public on the Home Front who gave the terrible weapon an odd superstar status. It was, after all, the war winning weapon they had been waiting for and the British public just couldn't get enough of the new machine. It was an excellent and forward thinking piece of engineering, but not quite the saviour they had been promised. The tank did not win the war, but it did succeed in opening up a war, leading to a renewed mobility for the Allies. On the whole the public were more or less oblivious to the tanks successes or its failures and lapped up as much hype they were given. Tank Banks toured the country raising money for the war effort and tank related souvenirs were eagerly snapped up by the veracious tank hungry public. Amongst these were photographs, stereo-views and postcards showing the tank in all its glory.

It is undeniable that the tank has changed the face of warfare forever; it has become a household name, a star and as with all the biggest stars, everywhere the tank went there was a photographer to record its triumphs and embarrassments for posterity. These images must number into the thousands and even now, over 90 years later, new, unseen photographs come to light on a regular basis. This book is the culmination of over 20 years of collecting and aims to show the evolution of the British Great War tank through some of the many thousands of original period images taken of this curious and contentious machine. The following pages show images of each mark of tank recorded by the factories that made them, the British army, the German army, civilians on holiday, artists and commercial photographers. Many of the images were deemed as being beyond Top Secret when originally taken and have never been published before.

These first primitive machines were unreliable, poorly armoured and a magnet for every enemy gun for miles around. The work of the photographers who recorded their first faltering steps onto the battlefield was invaluable. Now that Harry Patch, the last fighting Tommy, has passed away, the misery of the trenches of the Great War has gone forever from living memory and moved onto the pages of the history books. These images are a monument, a lasting and tangible link between the present day and the horror of tank warfare of over 90 years ago.

CHAPTER 1
PROTOTYPES

Since the start of the Great War in 1914 several forward thinking individuals and companies had been working on their ideas for an off-road armoured fortress. The Pedrail Landship, Elephants Feet, the Twin Bullock Creeping Grip, Hetherington's Big Wheel and the Killen-Strait Tractor were just a few of the more remarkable contenders. This chapter covers some of the more successful examples and those directly linked to the evolution of the tank

By 1899 the problem of Boer raids on British convoys in South Africa was becoming serious. In response, several Fowler Model B5 10 nhp steam traction engines were clad in steel plate and by 1900 they were in South Africa, along with their bullet proof wagons. In total, four *Fowler Armoured Trains* were made, but they were not universally appreciated by those asked to operate them and their impact on operations was limited

A works illustration of one of the first commercially successful tracked machines to go into production. It is taken from the factory catalogue for the American Killen-Strait of 1913-14. The arrow at the front tells the driver which way the front steering track is pointing. One of the first things the military changed was the canvas 'market stall' roof (Bill Baker)

The location here is the test area of the Talbot Motor Works in mid 1915. The two RNAS officers seen here obviously having a great time at the controls of the Killen-Strait are thought to be Major Thomas Hetherington and Lieutenant Colonel Albert Stern. Note the 1914 Admiralty Pattern Rolls Royce Armoured Car parked in the background.

The Killen-Strait being tested at the Talbot works at Barlby Road, London in 1915. This image clearly shows how manoeuvrable and rugged the machine was, but it was another dead-end in the evolution of the tanks

March 1915 saw the arrival in England of one of the first Killen Strait Tricycle Tractors to enter the country. It was touted around as being the first of the viable tank prototypes, but even with the addition of an old armoured car body it was never going to be a real contender (Tank Museum, Bovington)

The Foster-Hornsby 'Yukon' tractor of 1910 was never intended to be a prototype armoured fighting vehicle. However, the experience gained by William Foster and Co Ltd of Lincoln would serve them well five years later when they were asked to produce a Landship (Ray Hooley)

The impressive shape of the American Holt 75hp tractor. This machine was an excellent workhorse and was used for heavy haulage by the British army in France, Belgium and Mesopotamia. It is also often hailed by many as the basis for the first British tanks, but in actual fact it played no part whatsoever in the mechanical evolution of the tank (Ray Hooley)

A Hornsby 'Chain Track' tractor hauling heavy artillery for the British army on Salisbury Plain at sometime around 1910. When the new tractor was first demonstrated, many in the military dismissed it, as they said it would frighten the horses. Perhaps they were more worried that it would replace the horses?

A photograph showing a Rolls Royce Silver Ghost armoured car, with its cab and turret removed to show the armourment and firing position. The wheels were no good for trench crossing, the Landships Committee would need to forget about armoured cars and concentrate on tracked designs from now on

The menacing, but strangely elegant form of the 1914 Pattern Rolls Royce Armoured Car. Based on the running gear of the Silver Ghost, this vehicle served in one form or another well into the Second World War. No matter how good it was it was out of its depth when put against the mud and barbed wire strewn trenches of the Western Front

A rare and very useful view of the back of a Rolls Royce Armoured Car in the workshops and loaded with a fairly surly looking crew. Note the double rear wheel sets and large storage boxes

Many motor manufacturers and well-healed private individuals produced armoured cars during the Great War; some were better than others. This fabulous creation is the Seabrook 5 ton Armoured Lorry of late 1914, seen here on service with the Royal Naval Air Service.

Another view of a Seabrook Armoured Lorry, this time with un-battened hatches and a full crew. The Seabrook was built around a lorry from the American Standard Motor Truck Co of Detroit. It was armed with a 3.pdr gun and a single Vickers-Maxim.

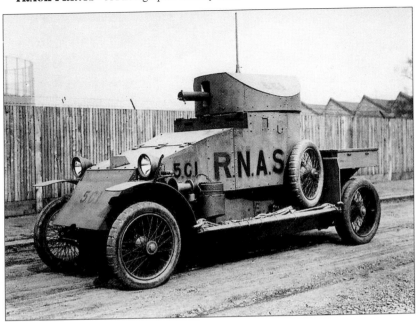

After the legendary Rolls Royce, one of the best Armoured Cars of the Great War was the Admiralty Pattern Lanchester of 1915. It was on similar lines to the Rolls Royce, had the same armourment and was just as manoeuvrable, but it was considerably lighter and cheaper to produce.

Fresh from the workshops of Stothern and Pitt of Bath, this photograph shows Colonel Cromptons fabulous but ill-fated Pedrail Landship. The Pedrail Landship was unveiled in July-August 1915 and was unfortunately a failure (Tank Museum, Bovington)

A close up view of the Pedrail Landship leaving the Stothern and Pitt works for the first time.

The Pedrail Landship clad in canvas instead of the intended armoured steel. The machine went through various trials and evaluations, but it was never going to be able to do what was being asked of it by the newly formed Landships Committee (Tank Museum, Bovington)

The Foster-Daimler 105hp heavy haulage tractor was designed especially for towing large guns destined for the siege of Paris. This huge tractor would prove invaluable in 1916 when Fosters produced their first Landships. Most of the running gear from the tractor was used in the Landships

A rarely seen view showing the rear of the Foster-Daimler 105hp Tractor. The rear wheels of this amazing machine were just over 8 feet tall.

Lincoln's South Common provides a testing trial for one of the 105hp tractors. This area was used for vehicle tests by most of Lincolns engineering establishments such as Ruston & Proctor and Clayton & Shuttleworth

A pair of Foster-Daimler tractors working together to tow the carriage for a massive siege gun

Three of the huge 105hp tractors take a break from their work. The barrel of the enormous gun they are moving can be seen to the left of the photograph

Foster-Daimler 105hp tractor number 33 undertaking its everyday tasks as a heavy haulage tractor in France. O.H.M.S. on the side of the box radiator stands for On His Majesties Service

Fosters heavy siege tractors lined up in the works yard awaiting delivery to the Admiralty

Foster 105hp tractor number 44 was lengthened and converted into the worlds first trench crossing machine as one of the early prototypes of the Landships project. It performed well, but was never going to be a viable trench breaking war winner

CHAPTER 2

· ● ·

THE LINCOLN NUMBER 1 MACHINE AND LITTLE WILLIE

The first of the serious tank prototypes was produced by William Foster and Co Ltd of Lincoln, England. The first attempt was the Lincoln Number 1 and it has serious failings, mainly that the commercially available tracks could not handle the increased weight or extra stresses. Once a set of purpose built tracks had been produced specially for the job, Little Willie was born and the way was open for the next step along the road to the first tanks.

In August 1915 the Lincoln Number 1 Machine started to take shape in the assembly shops of William Foster & Co Ltd in Lincoln. The Lincoln Number 1 would originally have a turret and be fitted with American tracks that soon proved to be no good for needs of the designers (Tank Museum, Bovington)

The Lincoln Number 1 Machine had a short life. By late 1915 it had been adapted to carry William Trittons all new pressed steel track and had lost its turret. In this final form, the machine was named Little Willie. The wheels at the rear are called the steering gear and proved near to useless for actually steering the vehicle.

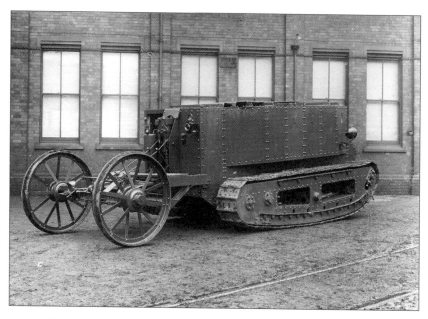

A splendid three quarter rear view of the brand new Little Willie as he stands proudly in the William Foster and Co works yard in Lincoln

Late 1915 saw Little Willie on test at Burton Park in Lincoln. The wood strapped to the track frames was apparently there to replicate the extra weight of guns and crew that the machine would have to carry if it had ever gone into production.

Little Willie did not go into production and never saw action, but was sent to several evaluations and tests during the war. This is Little Willie at the testing area at Dollis Hill. He is beginning to look extremely tatty and is obviously not being treated very well.

Thought to be at some time in the late 1930s, Little Willie is now missing his steering gear and looking very much the worse for wear. He is pictured here at the embryonic, outdoor Tank collection at Bovington Camp in Dorset.

By the 1970s Little Willie had been recognised as a unique and irreplaceable prototype tank and has been brought inside and given a coat of paint by the staff at the Tank Museum.

Here we see a rear view showing Little Willie amongst friends as he is today. His steering gear is now lost forever, but he has now been painstakingly restored and given pride of place on his own turntable in the newly created hall dedicated to the story of the tank at the Tank Museum, Bovington.

CHAPTER 3
MOTHER

When it first appeared, the next machine after Little Willie was officially designated as 'His Majesties Landship Centipede', but to everyone working on the project it soon became simply known as 'Mother'. This machine was the first tank and soon, Mothers armoured children would be earning their keep in France, Belgium and Mesopotamia

Little Willie had been a useful test-bed, but the staff in Fosters design office had continued working on their next design. On January 12th 1916 'Centipede' ran for the first time in Fosters works yard. Here Centipede is seen on test at Burton Park in Lincoln.

A splendid starboard view of Centipede on factory test in Burton Park on December 3rd 1916. The machine did all that was asked of it and instead of Centipede, it soon became known to everyone as 'Mother'.

Here we see Mother being sent over a trench in factory trials in Burton Park. The object of the exercise is partly to see if the tanks guns can be kept on target whilst crossing an obstacle. The target in this case being particularly vicious looking sandbags on strings.

Mother coming full tilt, straight up a steep hill towards the camera. Its creators, William Tritton and Walter Wilson can be seen disappearing off camera to the left. Mother had twice as many rivets as a production tank, so she is always easily recognisable

This grainy little snapshot is actually a very rare image showing Mother on her official military tests at Hatfield Park (Tank Museum, Bovington)

Mother was the first of the Great War tanks and deserved to take pride of place at Bovington early collection. Unfortunately the tank was systematically robbed for parts over the years until by the late 1930s she was a shadow of her former self (Tank Museum, Bovington)

Mother had been ill-treated over the years and soon after these last sad photographs were taken she was sliced up by the scrap-mans torch and lost forever (Tank Museum, Bovington)

CHAPTER 4
THE MARK I

Produced in Mothers image, the Mk I was the first of the true tanks and they were also an idea ahead of their time, but they were wasted by being put into battle in small numbers and on unsuitable ground. Even more tragic than this was that perhaps their greatest advantage, the element of surprise was squandered. Despite these problems, they paved the way for other, more technologically advanced machines and created the blueprint for tank operations to this day

One of the first tanks made in Mothers image being built in March 1916. This image is a bit of a mystery. Only Fosters are known to have built tanks in Lincoln, but the photo bears a military contract number given to Robey and Co, also of Lincoln. Note a second tank to the right of the shot (Ray Hooley)

A splendid three quarter view of the same William Foster or Robey built Mk I tank
(Ray Hooley)

Female workers or 'Munitionettes' plaining track shoes for tank production at
William Foster and Co Ltd in mid 1917. This would have been a full time job as 180 of
these shoes were needed for each side of every rhomboid tank that left the factory

Male Mk I, 743, is loaded onto a train in Lincoln in mid 1916. A substantial amount of the interior is taken up with the engine and transmission. The Russian script on the hull was supposed to support the cover story that the tanks were water carriers for the unmade roads of Mesopotamia and Russia.

Male and Female Mk I tanks lined up and ready, prior to their debut at Flers on 15th September 1916. The Male tanks carried three machine guns and a pair of 6 pound cannons, whereas the Female machines were equipped with five machine guns and no cannon.

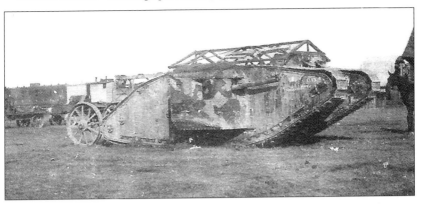

Lt. Sir John Dashwoods Mark I Male C. 13 photographed before the battle of Flers. Note the early camouflage scheme and the anti-grenade netting. The Mk I tanks had a similar steering gear arrangement as that fitted to Little Willie.

Tank C. 15 passes a group of entrenched infantry before the battle of Flers. The men seem unconcerned by the machine and are likely to be used to the activities of members of the Heavy Battalion Machine Gun Corps, the forerunners of the Tank Corps.

The cavalry saw no advantage in the mechanisation of the army and tried to discredit the tanks and their crews at every opportunity. This 1916 illustration from The Graphic magazine must have delighted those who fought to keep the horse, but lose the tank.

Female Mk I tank C.16 'Corunna' with the remains of Leuze Wood behind it. This tank was commanded at Flers by 2/Lt. Eric Purdy of the H.B.M.G.C. It is not known for sure what happened to the tank. It may have snapped a track or been hit by a shell, recent sources suggest that it may even have been a victim of a stray British shell.

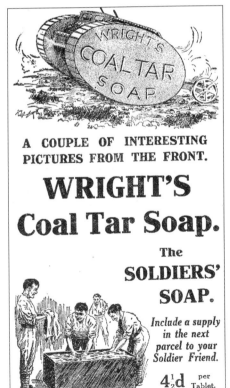

A COUPLE OF INTERESTING PICTURES FROM THE FRONT.

WRIGHT'S
Coal Tar Soap.

The
SOLDIERS'
SOAP.

Include a supply in the next parcel to your Soldier Friend.

$4\frac{1}{2}$d per Tablet.

The public fascination for the tanks started as soon the first descriptions of tanks were released in September 1916. Before long the tank would be the subject of songs, poems and would even end up advertising everything from War Bonds to soap.

A Female Mk I tank identified simply as 785. The Female Mk I tanks were made by the Metropolitan Carriage, Wagon and Finance Co of Birmingham. The date and location of this particular photograph is currently unknown to the author.

One of the survivors of the Battle of Flers was Female tank 504, Battalion number C. 6, known to the crew as Cordon Rouge. The tank is seen here driving back down the road to Albert and taking part in what is almost certainly a staged photo opportunity. It had been commanded in the battle by 2/Lt J. Allan H.B.M.G.C. (Tank Museum, Bovington)

Lincoln made Male Mk I tank D. 17 'Dinnaken' ditched on the battlefield after Flers. The tank had been commanded by Lt. S.H. Hastie of the Highland Light Infantry. Dinnaken had been forced to pull out of the battle due to engine problems.

Another view of Male MK I D. 17 'Dinnaken'. The tank stayed where it had been left for some considerable time acting as a forward command post for visiting officers. Dinnaken was later to be unceremoniously broken up for scrap by German prisoners of war.

The original caption for this fabulous image says that it shows *'Canadian infantry and their German prisoners being guided across the battlefield by a tank'*. In reality the Mk I in the shot has probably been ditched and sat there for some time.

Damaged Male Mk I C. 5 'Crème de Menthe' after the Battle of Flers. In November 1916 the Daily Mirror paid the Canadian Records Office the huge sum of £1000 for this image as it was the first photograph of a tank released to the British public.

Until the Daily Mirror had paid £1000 for the first photograph of a tank in action, most people had nothing else to go but the fanciful ideas of the postcard makers.

A photograph taken either at Bovington Camp or more likely at the Tank Corps Central Workshops near Erin in France. The tanks shown are for spares or repair and are mostly Mk IVs. In the foreground is Female Mk II 528. With the sponsons removed, the cramped interior of the machine is evident despite the poor quality of the photograph.

By the end of the war, relics from the tank battle at Flers still littered the battlefield. This image is taken from a post-war stereoview card and shows the remains of Male Mk I C1 'Champagne'. Note the early front idler sprockets with teeth the same as the rear drive sprockets; these were soon dropped as they caused undue wear to the tracks

CHAPTER 5
MARKS II AND III

Subtle changes to the original Mk I lead to the creation of the MkII and III machines. Primarily intended for training, they helped the fledgling crews hone their skills ready for battle and added safety features such as better escape hatches gave those crews half a fighting chance of survival should the worst happen

Queen Mary inspects a Female Mk II before taking a spin in the specially prepared and cleaned tank. King George V decided that he would also like a ride; in fact he thought that a tank race would be a good idea. However, the Kings tank was an unprepared model and he emerged afterwards a little worse for wear with a very grubby uniform.

A view of the back of a male Mk II tank captured intact at Bullecourt in April 1917. The main visual difference between the old Mk I and the new Mk II tanks was the removal of the near useless steering gear. The track extensions were there to help spread the tanks weight and were called 'Spuds'

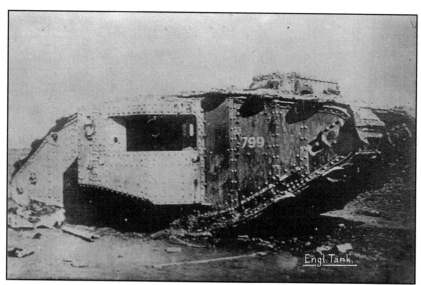

Male Mk II 779 captured intact after the Battle of Bullecourt. After their inspection the Germans concluded that they were unimpressed by the tank and blew it up with several boxes of gun cotton. Recently, many parts of the tank were excavated and can be seen by appointment at a private museum in Bullecourt.

This Female Mk II was captured intact after breaking both tracks at Bullecourt in April 1917. The Mk II tanks had been made for training only and their hulls were standard soft boilerplate instead of specially prepared 'armoured' steel. Despite this, Tank shortages meant that these soft skin tanks were sent into battle.

The same Female Mk II as captured in near pristine condition.

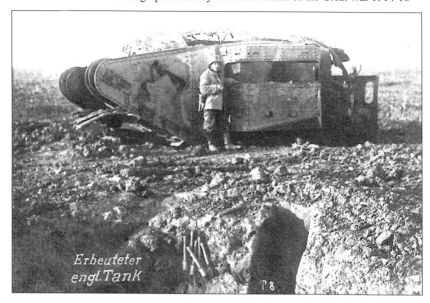

After its capture the unfortunate machine was used by German troops for anti-tank and grenade training. Note the terrific amount of damage inflicted by stick grenades long after the battle of Bullecourt had finished.

Yet another shot of the same Female Mk II on the battlefield at Bullecourt. The German flag in front is thought to mean that the wreck should not be removed as it is being used for training with live ammunition.

The German troops have now reduced most of the unfortunate Mk II to scrap; the entire rear end is now almost completely blown away.

A splendid photograph showing the same Female Mk II in context with the trenches it would have been attacking. This series of six photographs are just a few of the many taken of this particular tank by the specialist German photography teams.

Ditched somewhere on the battlefield after the Battle of Arras in April 1917. From this angle, the William Foster made Male Mk II, 790, appears quite intact and undamaged.

A very interesting shot of an old Mk II transformed into a supply carrying tank. The problem of getting supplies to the front was partially solved by using old tanks. Note how the guns have been removed and the sponson apertures have been plated over. The date and location of this image is unknown.

A Male Mk III being used for training on Wool Heath in mid 1917. The ramshackle collection of tents in the background is the beginnings of the Bovington Camp we know today (Tank Museum, Bovington)

CHAPTER 6
THE MK IV

In 1917 the Mk IV tanks were delivered ready for the renewed spring offensive in Flanders. The new machines were a huge improvement on those that had gone before, but these were still early days and, as with the Mk I tank at Flers, the Generals who directed the battles still had little idea of what a tank could and couldn't really do. Their appearance on the muddy morass of Ypres did them no favours at all. However, on 20th November 1917 the tanks and their crews got the chance they had been waiting for when they went into battle on the firm unbroken ground around Cambrai. The tank had come of age

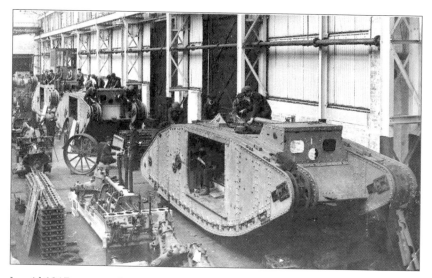

In mid 1917 a new tank started to be produced. This photograph shows the Erecting Shop at William Foster and Co Ltd in Lincoln and the tanks are the new Mk IV. With the introduction of the Mk IV the tank went from primitive, almost prototype machine to battle winner overnight.

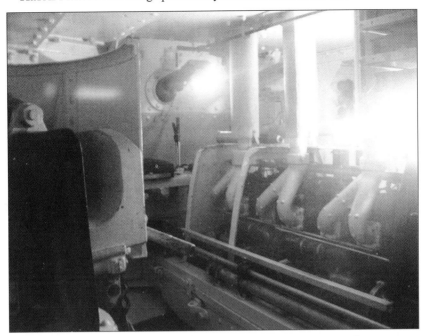

The interior of a Mk IV with the Daimler 105hp 'Silent Knight' engine taking up most of the available space. An eight man crew would have to cram themselves into the tank, whilst operating the guns, changing the gears, driving and trying to keep the engine running (Tank Museum, Bovington)

Sir William and Lady Tritton on the right of this photograph show various military dignitaries around a brand new Mk IV at the Foster tank testing ground in Lincoln

Tanks as far as the eye can see at the 'Tankodrome' near Erin in Northern France

Military dignitaries watch as a brand new Male Mk IV is tested on William Fosters 'Tank Testing Ground' in mid 1917. Note the Foster built tractors in the background. This area is now taken up by supermarkets and retail units (Bill Baker)

The Mk IV was sent into action for the first time at the Third Battle of Ypres in the summer of 1917. The tanks performed well enough, but the ground conditions were atrocious. Many tanks sank up to their sponsons in mud that would not have supported the weight of a man, let alone a 30 ton tank.

So many tanks were lost in the Flanders Campaign that the area around Hooge, Poelkapelle and Langemark gained the rather macabre nickname of '*The Cemetery of the Tanks*'.

This Male Mk IV is A2 'Almeda'. It was left in this condition after the fighting at Zillebeke in September 1917. According to some sources 'Almeda' was recovered, repaired and reissued as A2 'Abou-Ben-Adam' for the Battle of Cambrai in November of the same year.

Female Mk IV D1 'Druid' became bogged down in a roadside ditch near to Kerselaar on the 4th October 1917. It stayed there for some considerable time after the war and is often described as the most photographed tank of the Great War.

A brace of Female Mk IV's that almost blocked the road leading out of Poelkapelle after the fighting there in early October 1917. On the left is Lt. Butlers tank D32 'Dop Doctor' and on the right is D24 'Deuce of Diamonds' commanded by Lt. Grant. The Germans named this pair of tanks *'Das Tanktor zu Poelkapelle'* or *'The Tank Gate of Poelkapelle'*.

Mk IV tanks complete with brushwood Fascines loaded onto trains ready for the Battle of Cambrai, set to start on the 20th November 1917. The Fascines were to be dropped into the deep German trenches of the Hindenburg Line so that the tanks could cross more easily (Tank Museum, Bovington)

In the foreground is Female Mk IV G.21 'Grasshopper' and behind that is male Mk IV F.6 Feu d' Artifice. Both tanks were destroyed during vicious fighting in Bourlon Wood on 23rd November 1917. In the summer of 2008 fragments of F.6 were recovered by archaeologists working for the television programme 'The Trench Detectives'.

A rare image looking back across the destroyed interior of F.6 Feu d' Artifice. The tank was not blown up by German artillery, so the damage is likely to be the result of a charge set by the escaping crew in order to stop the machine falling into enemy hands.

The Tank Corps Roll of Honour taken from a post war edition of the Tank Corps Journal. Many of the men listed were lost in the fighting at Cambrai. Despite the high losses Cambrai was a terrific victory for the tanks and is still celebrated by the Royal Tank Regiment to this day.

A Male Mk IV with the distinctly Welsh name of G. II 'Glamorgan', seen here carrying well over 30 Canadian soldiers. This was not standard troop carrying procedure and is obviously a staged photo opportunity.

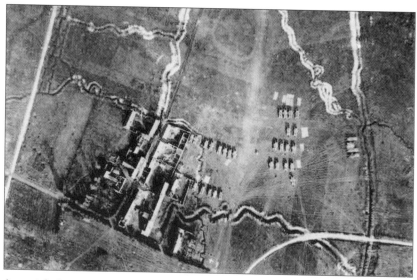

An aerial photograph taken somewhere in France showing Mk IV tanks in training for battle. The caption on the reverse states that it shows tanks at Ribecourt in late 1917, but this is unconfirmed(Bill Baker)

A Female Mk IV left on the Cambrai battlefield. The infantry in the foreground look as though they would rather be somewhere else and who can blame them? Identification of this tank is difficult, but it could be 'Esme', ditched in the Round Trench by Lt. Johnson on the 23rd November 1917.

A British postcard of the time showing the Cambrai tank attack from a German point of view. Fanciful stuff perhaps, but the huge, horrific shape of a tank bearing down on your trench must have been simply terrifying.

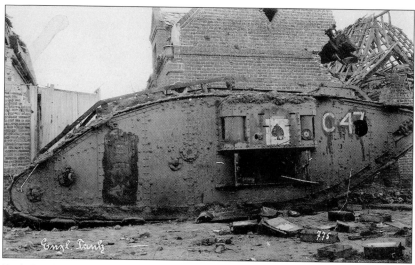

Tank C.47 'Conqueror II' lost at Fontaine-Notre-Dame. This tank has a rare example of 'Nose Art' more commonly seen on aircraft. The caricature is a string puppet German soldier shouting 'Kamerad'. After C47s capture, the caricature was painted out using old engine oil.

Female Mk IV 'F.W.1' was attached to the Wire Pulling Section at Cambrai. These specialist tanks towed a huge grapnel hook behind them as they ploughed through the barbed wire. F.W.1 was commanded by 2/Lt. C W Carles and was hit by artillery fire at Caron Farm near Rumilly on the 21st November.

In the foreground is Female Mk IV 'Eileen II' and behind her is male E3 'Eclipse II'. Both tanks were destroyed by German artillery on the plain of Moeuvres on the 23rd November. These were just two of six E Battalion tanks destroyed in this area.

The famous image shows the unfortunate male Mk IV H45 'Hyacinth' who was wedged fast and lost completely intact when his tail slid back down into a trench on the first day of the Battle of Cambrai.

The German tank salvage units became incredibly efficient in the retrieval and repair of damaged British tanks. This female Mk IV is I.36 'Invincible' captured intact by the Germans at Cambrai after retiring from the battle with a seized engine

Male Mk IV F41 'Fray-Bentos' was captured at Fontaine-Notre-Dame on the 27th November after mechanical problems. This photograph shows the tank being inspected by German officials in the Carre de Paille in Cambrai before going to Berlin.

After being captured 'Fray-Bentos' went by train to Berlin. Here it is seen being driven through Cambrai to the Railway Station. The red hand seen on the side of many F Battalion tanks was apparently made by the commander of the tank dipping his own hand in red paint and pressing it onto the side of his particular machine.

By 19th December 1917 'Fray-Bentos' was in Berlin and being inspected by crowds of German officers. At the front is the unmistakable figure of the Kaiser himself. After this brief brush with fame the tank was taken to Berlin Zoo along with other captured booty. It is thought that the tank was scrapped during World War Two.

From left to right are H48 'Hypathia', C53 'Coquette' and lastly H46 'Hyaena'. All three Female Mk IVs were lost on the 23rd November whilst trying to take Fontain-Notre-Dame. Missing from this image is H49 'High Flyer', having already been salvaged by the Germans.

Another casualty of the first day of Cambrai was Female Mk IV 'Hotspur II', knocked out, along with many other tanks, mainly from E Battalion, by the 77mm guns of the Feld-Artillerie-Regiment 108.

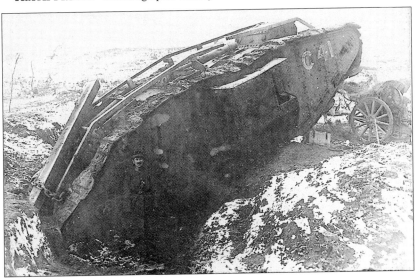

Male Mk IV C41 'Cherubim' lost a track whilst crossing the Hindenburg Line at Bantaux. This photograph was taken some time afterwards when the tank was being used as cover for a German 77mm gun. The mysterious German soldier appears in many of the Cambrai tank photographs and must have been one of the official photographers

A very impressive close up view of what is thought to be Ferocious III. This tank was hit in the starboard track on the 20th November, so this German official photograph must have been taken after its recovery and repair.

More heroic and stirring stuff from the postcard manufacturers, but this time proving that the German artists could be just as fanciful as the British ones.

War booty comes in many forms and after Cambrai the Germans had captured so many tanks that they started using them against their previous owners. This Female Mk IV tank could be H49 'High Flyer'.

Female Mk IV A10 'Antigone' has fallen into enemy hands after being lost on the 20th November, the first day of the Battle of Cambrai.

Another view of A10 'Antigone' lost near Marcoing Copse. Note the damage to the port side and the Lewis Gun magazines littering the area. This quite severe looking damage would be easily repaired by the German engineers

On the 20th November F22 'Flying Fox' attempted to cross the canal bridge at Masnieres. Damage to the bridge structure and the considerable weight of the tank led to the inevitable and the bridge collapsed beneath it.

Another view of the ill fated 'Flying Fox' and what remains of the Masnieres canal bridge. Two of the soldiers seen here on the carcass of the tank seem to be British or are at least wearing British uniforms?

It had been terrible decision to send the tank over the bridge, as this was the only crossing for miles. If the infantry and cavalry had been sent over first, things may have been different. To add insult to injury 'Flying Fox' was left in-situ as a support for a new wooden bridge built by German engineers.

Male Mk IV B28 'Black Arrow II' is seen here covered in snow a few days after being destroyed by fire from a pair of anti-aircraft lorries. The crews of K. Flak Batterie 7 accounted for seven tanks, blowing them to pieces one after another as they tried to enter Fontaine-Notre-Dame on the 23rd November. Almost all of the crews were killed and the action has become known as *The Day in Hell*

Two more tanks who felt full fury of 'The Day in Hell' were Female Mk IV B54 'Behemoth' in the foreground and B57 'Blarney Castle'. The Tank Corps officers and men killed in Fontaine-Notre-Dame on this terrible day are commemorated on the Louveral Memorial.

Tank B57 'Blarney Castle' had been caught up in the hail of fire at Fontaine-Notre-Dame on the 23rd November. It ended the day blocking the main road, on fire and with most of its crew dead. The tank was beyond repair, so the Germans scrapped it where it stood. Each rivet was broken by hand using large chisels and sledge hammers until the unfortunate machine was in its component parts and could be used for spares or ballistics testing

The identity of this Male Mk IV is currently unknown, although the photograph was certainly taken in the aftermath of the Battle of Cambrai. The works production number 4031 can clearly be seen, but the name and battalion are a mystery.

German soldiers march past a sight which must have made them feel slightly less worried about the threat of the British tanks. This female Mk IV has either had a direct hit from a very large calibre Howitzer or has been purposely destroyed by British engineers

The U.S.A. entered the war in 1917 and many of them saw the potential of the tank immediately. Here a group of young American officers inspect a Female Mk IV, thought to have been knocked out near Hooge in the summer of 1917

This image is a mystery and any suggestions would be gratefully accepted. The soldiers are Royal Artillery, but is the wooden Mk IV a training tank, is it one of the dummy machines used to confuse the Germans during the Battle of Cambrai or is it a prop for a concert party show? I suspect it is the last option.

Great War tanks did not restrict themselves only to the Western Front. This image shows 'Tiger' and 'Lady Wingate' amongst others being used to bolster the Egyptian Expeditionary Force in early 1918. Their success here was limited, to say the least, due mainly to the rigours of the sandy landscape.

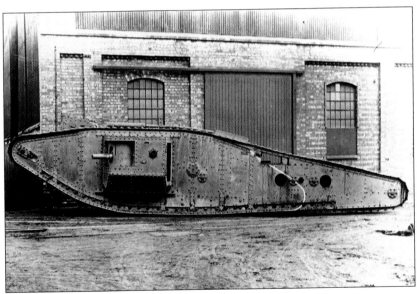

As the German trenches became wider, the British thought they should have a longer tank. This is a Male Mk IV fitted with a 'Tadpole Tail' attachment. Many sets of these were shipped to France but they were never used as they made the tank twist and almost impossible to steer (Tank Museum, Bovington)

A Female Mk IV with a Tadpole Tail shows off by towing a field gun and limber across rough ground.

As previously mentioned, the German army captured many British tanks at Cambrai and once repaired and repainted, used them against their previous owners. Here a Female Mk IV is paraded in front of German military dignitaries. Note the other two tanks parked in the background, ready to take their turn.

An almost completely destroyed captured Mk IV as used by the Germans in their attack on the French army near Reims.

This image shows a captured British Tank looking out menacingly across the battlefield whilst a lone aeroplane passes by. This shot is far too perfect and has probably been staged, perhaps even done after the war for a film? (Bill Baker)

Probably taken intact at Cambrai, Female Mk IV 2829 will now be repainted and used by the Imperial German Army.

The German answer to the British tanks was the much maligned A7V. It had an 18 man crew and was quite unstable on rough ground, but these were still early days. This tank is 504 'Schnuck' which was captured intact at Fremicourt in late August 1918. Unfortunately, it was scrapped in 1919 with only the 57mm cannon being saved.

This German owned Mk IV has come to grief in an attack on the Fort de Pompelle to the south of Reims in late 1918. It stayed there for some considerable time as a tourist attraction and the visitors would usually add their names or a message to the side of the tank

The tanks inventors and manufacturers back in England must have been horrified that their creations were being used by the enemy, but images like this must have made them feel better.

The tanks were hailed as such a success by the British public that they would soon tour much of the country as the Tank Banks. Here, the great and the good of Nottingham appeal for people to buy War Savings Certificates and War Bonds.

To be photographed doing your bit at one of the Tank Banks would have been a great honour.

A great deal of pomp and circumstance always accompanied the Tank Banks as they went about their curious work. Male Mk IV 130 'Nelson' was sent to York and got a fairly standard civic reception.

This photograph shows the crowds that formed around E26 'Egbert II' who was selling war bonds in London's Trafalgar Square. Egbert II was a terrific draw for the crowds as he had seen action at Cambrai and had the scars to prove it.

A close up view of the most popular of the tank banks, Egbert II. His battle scars were just what the public wanted to see and wherever he went people crowded around to see him and buy War Bonds from the girls who would set up their temporary office in his sponsons

The War Weapons Week at Walsall is the Tank Banks destination this time. The public fascination for the new weapon is evident from the huge crowds in attendance.

In their short career the tanks had done their bit on the Western Front, the Home Front and in the desert. In early 1918 the Tank Corps started work on a new front by going to America. A brand new Female Mk IV 'Britannia' was sent to raise money for War Bonds and stir up enthusiasm for the war, thus increasing American enlistment.

The crew of Britannia put her through her paces for the American crowds. Making tanks balance on their centre of gravity like this was not just a Tank Corps parlour trick; it was part of their basic driver training.

Wherever the tanks went, they attracted incredible attention from all those present. The people of The U.S.A. were to be no different, where it seemed as though every rivet was under close scrutiny.

Just why Britannia found herself covered in Nurses at one point during her transatlantic jaunt is unclear, but it certainly made for a terrific photo opportunity. One of the crew can be seen sitting on the cab.

The crew of Britannia gained considerable fame as they toured the States. Here some of the crew are photographed with local VIPs.

Britannia toured each town on her trip under her own power, but in-between she travelled by specially prepared railway wagon. Here she is loaded and ready or the off, note the spares at the front including a pair of new drive sprockets.

E42.

Here we see Britannia on a civilian snapshot sneakily taken over an American Railway Station wall.

Britannia and her crew were asked to do some fairly curious things whilst in the states. Perhaps one of the strangest was to run over a perfectly good wooden replica Mk IV tank.

Damaged and burnt out tanks littered the battlefields of the Western Front until well into the 1930s. Here a trio of tourists take a break to look at a German used Female Mk IV near the Fort de Pompelle.

The same group of tourists give us a useful rear view of the same tank.

Tanks were not only used as monuments on the battlefields of France and Belgium. A total of 265 old tanks were given away to towns and cities that had done well in raising money for the war effort. This Female Mk IV was presented to Cheltenham in 1919.

The municipal park in Barnoldswick suddenly found itself 'enhanced' by a Male Mk IV tank, training number 144. Not surprisingly, these Presentation Tanks were not universally appreciated and by the end of the Second World War only one of them still existed, it can still be seen in the High Street of Ashford in Kent.

William Foster made Male Mk IV 2332 on display in Ypres after the Great War. It stayed on show here until the town was occupied by the German army in the Second World War. One of the first things the invading German army did was to remove and destroy the towns old tank.

Another of William Fosters Lincoln made tanks displayed down the road from Ypres in the pretty little town of Poelcapelle. D29 'Damon II', production number 2380 was lost in the Third Battle of Ypres in 1917 and stood proudly in the town until the Germans arrived for a second time. In 1941 they took it away for scrap.

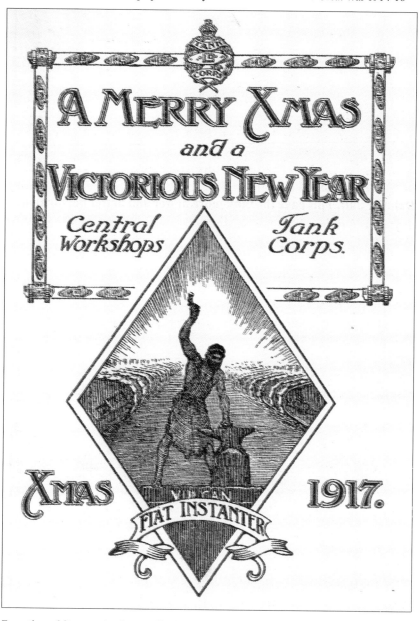

Even the soldiers at the front still celebrated Christmas. Here the Tank Corps wishes a Merry Christmas for 1917 and a victorious New Year for 1918, very prophetic indeed.

CHAPTER 7
THE MARK V

The Mk V arrived in France in 1918 and soon began to prove its worth. The 'Big Push' of August 1918, better known as the Battle of Amiens finally got the Germans on the run. The new tank had a purpose built Ricardo engine with 150hp instead of the old 105hp Daimler unit. This gave the tank more power and better performance, but lead to much higher operating temperatures inside the fighting compartment. The infantry was ably supported by the new Mk V at Amiens and once the Mk V had helped regain the armies lost mobility, there was no looking back

An excellent view showing a pair of pristine Mk V tanks on peace keeping duties in Cologne in 1919. These new tanks arrived in France in January of 1918 and perhaps their finest hour came just 6 month later in the Battle of Amiens.

As always, the tanks drew a crowd wherever they went and their arrival in Cologne was to be no exception.

The Tank Corps parade at the steps of Colognes famous Cathedral, much to the fascination of the town's citizens.

An unfortunate Male Mk V has become stuck in the mud of the Western Front and is awaiting assistance from a colleague.

A Mk V adapted into a crane proves its worth at Central Workshops in France (Tank Museum, Bovington)

A Mk V* either on training in England or being displayed for military top brass

A pristine Mk V* with the American army. Unfortunately, little is known of this image, so the age and exact location are a mystery, although the car in the background looks like a typical 1930s saloon. It is also unclear if the tank is still being used by the U.S. or if it is a museum piece or Gate Guard.

A Mk V tank, given to the White Russians after the Great War, is inspected by a second generation of Germans as they sweep through the Ukraine in 1942.

CHAPTER 8
THE MEN BEHIND THE GUNS

The tanks were a splendid and forward thinking piece of engineering, but without a knowledgeable, brave and dedicated crew, a tank would never get anywhere. Many leading officers in the army could see no real use for the tanks and campaigned at every opertunity to scrap the tanks, disband the Tank Corps and return the men to their units. The men of the Tank Corps were pioneers who fought, not only against the might of the German army, but also against narrow minds and red tape at home. Their victories on the battlefield bolstered their reputation and soon there was no question of their being disbanded. These photographs show just a few of the ordinary and often unidentified faces behind the tanks

A few of the ordinary faces usually hidden behind the steel walls of a tank. This photograph was taken in mid 1916 and shows men of the Heavy Battalion Machine Gun Corps. Standing in the centre with the moustache is Sergeant Charles Parrot M.M.

By early 1918 Sergeant Parrot was in the Tank Corps and home on leave. Unfortunately, the identity of the lady with Sgt. Parrot is unknown.

A 1918 dated photograph showing an unidentified Tank Corps private. There is no message on the reverse of this postcard, so the identity of the sitter and the date and location of the image will always be a mystery

Simply signed *'Love from Jack H.B.M.G.C, 1916'.* Unless anyone reading this book recognises him, we will never know who Jack was.

There is no name on this image, but in his message he says *'.....we are getting on well with the new buses, I will tell you all about them the next time I'm home'.* Buses was accepted military slag of the time for tanks and the soldier is likely to be an early member of the H.B.M.G.C.

A wonderful view of three British Great War soldiers, taken in early 1918. The reverse says *'To Will and Mary, from Harold R.A.M.C, Tom R.E. and Arthur Tank Corps'.* As is usual with Tank Corps personnel, Arthur is justly proud of his Tank Corps arm patch and has made sure that it is in prime position for the photograph

The crew of one of the famous Tank Banks getting the machine in place and ready for the days events. These Tank Banks raised millions of pounds for the war effort and helped secure the public fascination for the new machine

A fascinating photograph showing men of the H.B.M.G.C. or Heavy Branch-Machine Gun Corps. The image was taken before the issue of the distinctive tank shaped trade badge which started to appear on the upper right arm of tank crews in May 1917

Robert Stanley Britten joined the Tank Corps in July 1918. He had been in a reserved occupation as a policeman before he joined up and was not free to enlist for military service. To make up for this, as soon as he got a chance to join up he put his name down for the most dangerous job in the army and became a tank driver. Robert Britten survived the war and stayed in the army until leaving at the age of 42 in 1938

CHAPTER 9
THE MEDIUM A 'WHIPPET'

The rhomboid machines put against the trenches to this point had been known as 'The Heavies'. Their role was to flatten the barbed wire, smash the guns and break the trenches, but then what? Once the trenches were broken the need would be for a faster, medium machine, known at the time as a chaser. This was the role of the Medium A Whippet. At Amiens in August 1918, the trenches were broken by the heavy Mk V tanks and then the Whippets went in to exploit their advances

By the summer of 1917 something very different had been dreamed up by the design team at Fosters in Lincoln. This photograph shows their latest machine, which went by many names. It was either the Tritton Chaser, the Medium A or the Whippet (Tank Museum, Bovington)

The new tank, eventually called the Medium A Whippet, being built on the production line in Lincoln. A total of 200 were made before the armistice, all by Fosters. It was intended as a chaser tank and could do twice the speed of a Mk IV at around 7mph.

Brand new Whippet A302 takes time out from training to acquaint itself with the French civilians at Berck-Plage

The scene on the Foster tank testing ground in mid 1918. It is mostly populated by Medium A Whippets, but there is at least one Mk IV and a solitary 105hp Heavy Haulage Tractor

As with the Mk IV and V tanks, several Medium A tanks were captured by the Germans. This machine gives an impressive show for its new German owners.

An artists rendition of the Battle of Amiens showing Medium A Whippets leading the Highlanders and the Royal Flying Corps into the fray. The tanks camouflage scheme is purely artistic licence.

As with any of the other Great War tanks, the Whippet was a soft target for enemy artillery. This machine has been destroyed on the battlefield and gives a photo opportunity for an American 'Doughboy'.

Although this Medium A Whippet looks like it has been blown up it is in fact being stripped for parts at Tank Corps Central Workshops at Erin.

After the Great War, many Medium A Whippets were sold or given away to several of the world armies including the Japanese and as seen here in service Russian.

Medium A Whippets proceeding in a line across country. Note the huge amount of stores, track extension spuds and petrol cans hanging off the last machine (Tank Museum, Bovington)

CHAPTER 10
THE MEDIUM B AND THE MEDIUM C

With the breaking of the trenches, the heavies were all but out of a job. The phasing out of the heavy rhomboid tanks from 1918-19 was finalised, but replacements would still be needed. The Medium A was the first of the new generation and it was soon followed by the Medium B and C machines

Major Walter Wilson had been half of the inspired design team who created the first tanks at Fosters in 1916. Here, Walter Wilson, in uniform, exits his latest creation, the Medium B. Unfortunately, the tank was a poor design, which was quite out of character for Wilson (Tank Museum, Bovington)

When the White Russians asked for assistance from Britain after the war, we sent them several used Medium B machines such as this one. This seems to be uncharacteristically nice of the British government and was perhaps only done because the British army were so unhappy with the tank? (Tank Museum, Bovington)

Often described as the finest tank of the war, the Medium C Hornet was another tank from the William Foster stable in Lincoln. In actual fact the Medium C arrived just too late for the fighting and so should instead be described as the best tank never to see action.

A very useful head-on view of the Medium C Hornet on the William Foster and Co Ltd Tank Testing Grounds in Lincoln. No Male version of the tank was produced, although the drawings for the male variant were completed by Fosters drawing office.

A seldom seen view of the rear of the Medium C. The tank was used in the troubles in Northern Ireland just after the Great War, but never saw any service elsewhere. The last Medium C Hornet went out of service in 1928 and there are no known surviving examples left in the world.

A brace of Medium C Hornets race each other whilst firing blanks at the Royal Tournament in 1926.

The men of the Tank Corps march proudly through London during peace celebrations in 1919, followed by their latest and best tank, The Medium C Hornet.

The Tank Corps and their Medium C Hornets cross over the Thames on way through London during the post war peace celebrations

Medium C Hornets parade for VIPs at Aldershot in 1923. Note the semaphore device on the roof of each tank.

For anyone still in doubt over the fact that William Foster and Co Ltd of Lincoln invented the tank, this huge banner was commissioned and hung from the overhead crane in the factories Turning Shop for many years.

A modern day St. George slays the German dragon in this curious, but excellent old postcard

CHAPTER 11
THE MK IX

It wasn't just thousands of tins of Bully Beef and gallons of rum that needed to be regularly delivered to the men in the trenches. Petrol, medical supplies, ammunition, tons of wood, thousands of feet of barbed wire and water were just a few of the other essentials that needed to be moved around in huge quantities on a daily basis. The Mk IX was the first purpose built, dedicated supply tank. In addition to this, it will always have the honour of being the worlds first amphibious tank

The worlds first purpose built supply tank was the Mk IX made by Marshall Sons and Co of Gainsborough in Lincolnshire. It could carry stores or troops and one was even transformed into the worlds first fully equipped armoured battlefield ambulance (Tank Museum, Bovington)

A useful side view of the Mk IX supply tank

The Mk IX was used for several experiments including being turned into the worlds first amphibious tank (Tank Museum, Bovington)

A fabulous shot showing the floating Mk IX in the water, there are rumours that it eventually sank, although nobody seems quite sure (Tank Museum, Bovington)

J3.

The only surviving example of the Mk IX supply tank as it appears today in the Tank Museum collection at Bovington.

K1.

CHAPTER 12
THE MK VIII OR LIBERTY TANK

In 1917, America entered the war and they were quick to realise the potential of the tank. Soon an Anglo-American tank design had been finalised and Mk VIII, or the Liberty Tank as it became known, was born. Armed with a pair of six-pound cannon and seven machine-guns, the tank was not only an excellent design, it was a potent demonstration of trust, friendship and engineering prowess between England and America

Although this tank is usually credited as being an American machine, it was in fact an Anglo-American project. The Mk VIII or Liberty Tank as it is best known, was a huge machine powered by a V12 Liberty aircraft engine.

It was a shame that the Liberty tank never saw action as just one look at it would have been enough to make most people surrender.

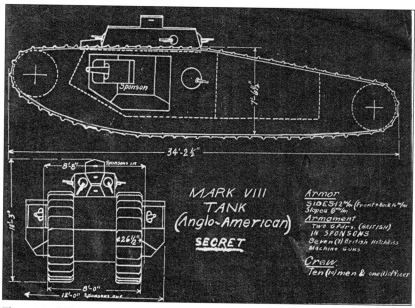

The original blueprints for the Mk VIII tank help to give an idea of its massive scale.

CHAPTER 13
THE GUN CARRIER

Mobile machine-guns inside an armour plated tank were a very useful thing to have on the battlefield, but once the trenches were broken a mobile artillery piece would be even more desirable. Horses and mules would usually be employed for towing heavy artillery around, but this was not only slow, complicated and unpredictable, it was becoming old fashioned and impracticable. With the unveiling of the Gun Carrier Mk I, the desire for fast field-gun delivery on any terrain became a reality. Suddenly a fully operational 6-inch Howitzer could be sent to any part of the battlefield, no matter how poor the ground conditions were

Not a true tank, rather a self propelled artillery piece instead. This is the Mk I Gun Carrier that started to arrive in France in June 1917. The prototype had first appeared at the Oldbury Tank Trials on the 3rd March 1917.

The Gun Carrier Tanks were based on running gear stripped from old Mk I tanks and even kept the steering gear, dropped from standard machines in late 1916. The Mk II version of the Gun Carrier never went further than the drawing board, but as it had been proposed the old machines were designated as Mk Is.

A rear view of the Mk I Gun Carrier on display at the Dollis Hill testing ground near Willesden, London. The photograph was taken late in or just after the war. Note the sheeted over Tadpole tailed Mk IV in the background

The Gun Carriers were all made by Kitsons of Leeds who had received an order for 50 such machines to be built immediately. They were powered by the 105hp Daimler engine and were intended as mobile artillery to be used after the trenches had been broken and the war became mobile again.

The gun Carriers were equipped with either a 5-inch field gun or a 6-inch howitzer. Two Gun Carrier companies were formed in July 1917 with twenty-four machines each. It is unlikely that any of them were ever used for their intended purpose and most spent their time being used as supply tanks.

BIBLIOGRAPHY, RECOMMENDED READING AND ACKNOWLEDGEMENTS

Anon.   1945   *A Short History of the Royal Tank Corps*
                             Gale and Polden LTD, Aldershot

Anon.   2007   *Mechanical Maintenance of the Mark IV Tank*
                             Friends of the Lincoln Tank, Lincoln

Baccarne R.   2008   *Poelcapelle 1917; A Trail of Wrecked Tanks*
                             Privately Published in Belgium

Beddows K.   1999   *Metro-Cammell, 150 years of Craftsmanship*
C & S Wheeler   K Beddows, C Wheeler, S Wheeler
                             and Runpast Publishing

Boin W.R.   1997   *War Memoirs 1917-19*
                             H.Karnac Books Ltd, London

Clark R.H.   1998   *Steam Engine Builders of Lincolnshire*
                             Society for Lincolnshire History
                             and Archaeology

Cooper B.   1974   *Tank Battles of World War I*
                             Ian Allan Ltd, Shepperton

Fletcher D.   1984   *Landships. British Tanks of the First World
                             War* - HMSO, London

Fletcher D.   1991   *Mechanised Force, British Tanks between the
                             Wars* - HMSO, London

Fletcher D.   1994   *Tanks and Trenches*
                             Sutton Publishing, Stroud

Fletcher D.   2001   *The British Tanks 1915-19*
                             Crowood Press, Ramsbury, Marlborough

Forty G. & A.   1988   *Bovington Tanks*
                             Dorset Publishing Company, Sherborne,
                             Dorset

Forty G.   1989   *Royal Tank Regiment, A Pictorial History*
                             Guild Publishers

William Foster   1920   *The Tank, Its birth and development*
and Co LTD   Bemrose and Sons, Derby
                             and London

Gibot J.L.   1999   *Following the Tanks, Cambrai*
Gorczynski P.   Imprimerie Centrale de l'Artois, Arras

Glanfield J.   2001   *The Devils Chariots*
                             Sutton Publishing, Stroud

Guderian H.   1999   *Achtung Panzer!*
                             Brockhampton Press

Hammond B.   2009   *Cambrai 1917; The Myth of the First
                             Great Tank Battle*
                             Weidenfeld and Nicholson, London

Holmes R.   1999   *The Western Front*
                             BBC Worldwide Ltd, London

Holmes R.   2008   *Shots from the Front; The British Soldier
                             1914-18* - Harper Press, London

Hundleby M   2009   A New A7V Tank
                             Lancfile Publishing, Lincs

Lane M.R.   1997   *The Story of the Wellington Foundry, Lincoln*
                             Unicorn Press, London

Liddell Hart B.H.   1934   *The History of the World War 1914-1918*
                             Faber and Faber LTD, London

Liddell Hart B.H.   1959   *The Tanks. The history of the Royal Tank
                             Regiment Volumes I and II*
                             Cassell and Co LTD, London

The Lincoln Tank 1988   *Tank Papers*
Group   *Moorprint, Lincoln*

Macksey K.   1988   *Tank versus Tank*
                           Guild Publishing

Mitchell F.   1987   *Tank Warfare*
                           Spa Books, Stevenage

Parker C. &   2000   *Aircraft Made in Lincoln*
Walls J   Society for Lincolnshire History
                           and Archaeology

Pidgeon T.   1995   *The Tanks at Flers. Volumes I and II*
                           Fairmile Books, Surrey

Peglar M.   1982   *The Tank Corps. Honours and Awards*
                           1916-1919 - Midland Medals, Birmingham.

Pullen R.   2006   *Tanks of the Great War; The Colouring Book*
                           Tucann Design and Print, Heighington, Lincs

Pullen R.   2008   *Beyond the Green Fields*
                           Tucann Design and Print, Heighington, Lincs

Pullen R.   2009   *The Landships of Lincoln*
                           (Reprint) Tucann Design and Print,
                           Heighington, Lincs

Reynolds J.   1999   *Engines and Enterprise, The Life and Work of*
                           Sir Harry Ricardo - Sutton Publishing, Stroud

Rigby W.   1923   *The evolution of the Tank*
                           Unpublished Article held by Lincoln City
                           Archives

Ruston and   1920   *Our Part in the Great War*
Hornsby Ltd   Bemrose and Sons, Derby and London

Schneider W &   1990   *German Tanks in World War I. The A7V and*
Strasheim R   *Early Tank Development*
                           Schiffer Publishing, Pennsylvania

Smithers A.J.   1986   *A New Excalibur*
                               Book Club Associates

Stern A.   1919   *Tanks 1914-1918, The Logbook of a Pioneer*
                               Richard Clay and Sons, London

Swinton E.D.   1932   *Eyewitness*
                               Hodder and Stoughton Limited, London

White B.T.   1978   *British Tank Markings and Names*
                               Squadron/Signal Publications, Michigan

Whitmore M.   1989   *Mephisto. A7V Sturmpanzerwagen 506*
                               Queensland Museum, Brisbane, Australia

Wilson A.G.   1986   *Walter Wilson: Portrait of an Engineer*
                               Gerald Duckworth and Co Ltd, London

Wright P.   2000   *Tank, the progress of a monstrous
                               war machine* - Faber and Faber, London

Additional material and assistance was supplied by;
The Tank Museum, Bovington
Tony Ablett
Bill Baker
Ray Hooley
Philippe Gorczynski
Chris Gresham
The Lincolnshire Echo Newspaper

Unless otherwise stated all material including photographs and other images used within this book are from the collection of the author.